YOU MUST REMEMBER THIS

1933

MILESTONES, MEMORIES,
TRIVIA AND FACTS, NEWS EVENTS,
PROMINENT PERSONALITIES &
SPORTS HIGHLIGHTS OF THE YEAR

TO :

FROM :

MESSAGE :

*selected and researched
by
betsy dexter*

WARNER ⓦ TREASURES™
PUBLISHED BY WARNER BOOKS
A TIME WARNER COMPANY

COPYRIGHT © 1996 BY
WARNER BOOKS, INC.
All Rights Reserved.

Warner Books, Inc.
1271 Avenue of the Americas
New York, New York 10020

Warner Treasures is a
trademark of Warner Books, Inc.

W A Time Warner Company

DESIGN:
CAROL BOKUNIEWICZ DESIGN
PRINTED IN SINGAPORE
FIRST PRINTING: SEPTEMBER 1996
10 9 8 7 6 5 4 3 2 1
ISBN: 0-446-91145-3

Franklin Delano Roosevelt

It was the year President **Franklin Delano Roosevelt** took office pledging to restore faith in the nation's economy. FDR declared a national bank holiday, suspending the activity of the Federal Reserve System and all

newsreel

the national guard

was made part of the United States Army in wartime and national emergencies.

banks. In his first radio Fireside Chat, the president encouraged the public to have confidence in the country's currency and banks. "The only thing we have to fear," FDR declared, "is fear itself."

SCIENTISTS IN MASSACHUSETTS REPORTED THAT SENATORS' BRAINS WEIGHED AN AVERAGE OF TWO OUNCES MORE THAN THOSE OF REPRESENTATIVES.

On March 10, at 5:55 in the afternoon, a violent earthquake hit Long Beach, CA, killing 123 people and wounding more than 4,150. Sixteen aftershocks and countless fires kept Los Angeles and Orange County in a state of terror for weeks.

the illinois waterway

opened, linking the Great Lakes and the Gulf of Mexico.

J. P. MORGAN, THE NATION'S RICHEST MAN, REVEALED BEFORE A SENATE COMMITTEE THAT HE HADN'T PAID TAXES IN YEARS.

THE TWENTY-FIRST AMENDMENT TO THE CONSTITUTION, REPEALING PROHIBITION, WAS RATIFIED.

Adolf Hitler became Chancellor of Germany.

The Nazis burned the Reichstag and accused the Communists of setting the fire. The German government outlawed freedom of the press, all labor unions, and all political parties, except the Nazis. The Gestapo began hunting down, shooting, and jailing government opponents. By March, the transporting of Jews to concentration camps had begun. In July, Hitler announced a law to "purify the German race."

international headlines

In Jaffa, more than 20 persons were killed and 130 wounded, as police clashed with Arabs protesting Jewish immigration to Palestine.

THE SPANISH GOVERNMENT SUPPRESSED INSURRECTIONS BY ANARCHISTS IN BARCELONA AND OTHER CITIES.

Austria outlawed the wearing of any political party uniforms.

In Norway, **Vidkun Quisling** resigned as minister of defense and formed the Nasjonal Samling (National Union) Party, dedicated to the suppression of Communism and Unionism.

Calling her a "boon to womanhood," **mae west** was honored by the country's obstetricians and gynecologists for popularizing the plump figure.

Mae West

DIEGO RIVERA was fired from the Rockefeller Center murals project. The Mexican painter would not agree to remove a small head of Lenin from the painting and the entire mural was destroyed.

Chicago residents were proud to play host to the World's Fair. Highlights included the unveiling of Grant Wood's painting *American Gothic* and Sally Rand's fan dance.

LINCOLN KIRSTEIN AND GEORGE BALANCHINE, DANCE INNOVATORS, FOUNDED THE **SCHOOL OF AMERICAN BALLET.**

In Germany, all books by Jewish and non-Nazi authors were ordered burned. Modern art was suppressed in favor of so-called "realism."

albert einstein was deprived of his German citizenship and later settled in Princeton, NJ.

cultural
milestones

The country's very first "Men's Magazine," ***esquire,*** began publication this year. Its claim to fame was risqué photos of scantily clad women.

FDR APPOINTED THE NATION'S FIRST WOMAN CABINET MEMBER, **FRANCES PERKINS.** SHE WAS SELECTED TO HEAD UP THE DEPARTMENT OF LABOR.

most popular new shows

"The Romance of Helen Trent," starring Virginia Clark

"Jack Armstrong, the All-American Boy," starring St. John Terrell

"Don McNeill's Breakfast Club"

"The Lone Ranger," starring George Seaton and John Todd

"Ma Perkins," starring Virginia Payne

"The Jimmy Durante Show"

radio

top radio performers

1. Eddie Cantor
2. Bing Crosby
3. Kate Smith
4. Jack Pearl
5. Guy Lombardo's Orchestra
6. Lowell Thomas
7. Ed Wynn
8. Rubinoff
9. Gracie Allen
10. Rudy Vallee

Eddie Cantor

Perpetually 39-year-old comedian **jack benny** got the longest laugh in radio history for his immortal reply to a stickup man's demand: "Your money or your life!" After a drawn-out pause, the comic responded: "I'm thinking it over."

Jack Benny

PREMIUM FEVER

struck this year, as listeners busily clipped boxtops to send in for gewgaws of their favorite radio shows.

The Federal Radio Commission became the Federal Communications Commission (FCC).

Hollywood hoofer extraordinaire **FRED ASTAIRE,** 34, married prominent Manhattan socialite and divorcée **PHYLLIS LIVINGSTON BAKER POTTER,** 25, in a star-studded ceremony.

milestones
celeb weddings of the year

Movie star **GARY COOPER, 32,** married **VERONICA BALFE,** a 20-year-old actress, in Manhattan.

MAX SCHMELING, ONE-TIME HEAVYWEIGHT CHAMPION, MARRIED CZECH MUSICAL COMEDY AND CINEMA ACTRESS **ANNY ONDRA,** IN BERLIN.

DEATHS

Calvin Coolidge, the 30th president, died in Northampton, ME, January 5. When informed of his death, Dorothy Parker quipped, "How can you tell?"

Fatty Arbuckle, Hollywood comic actor forced out of the biz by a manslaughter scandal, died June 29 in Los Angeles at 46.

James "Gentleman Jim" Corbett, boxer, died February 18 at 66 in New York. Corbett took the heavyweight crown from John L. Sullivan.

Robert Chesebrough, the American chemist who invented Vaseline, died September 8 at 96. He attributed his longevity to a daily spoonful of his own petroleum jelly.

Jimmie Rodgers, the "Singin' Brakeman," died May 26 in New York. Called the father of modern country music, Rodgers was considered the best yodeler in the business. He was 35.

Ring Lardner, much-loved author of stories about the common man, died in East Hampton, NY, September 25 at 48.

births

MICHAEL CAINE, prolific English actor who won an Oscar for *Hannah and Her Sisters*, was born in London March 14.

WILLIE NELSON, freewheeling country singer, was born April 30 in Abbott, TX.

LARRY KING, CNN interview whiz, was born November 19 in New York City.

ROMAN POLANSKI, director of *Rosemary's Baby*, was born August 18 in Paris.

PHILIP ROTH, author of *Portnoy's Complaint*, was born March 19 in Newark, NJ.

JOHNNY UNITAS, the recordbreaking quarterback of the Baltimore Colts, was born March 7 in Pittsburgh, PA.

F. LEE BAILEY, the flamboyant attorney who's defended everyone from Patty Hearst to O. J. Simpson, was born in Waltham, MA, June 10.

'33

hit music

- **you're getting to be a habit with me** Bing Crosby
- **forty-second street** Don Bestor
- **stormy weather** Leo Reisman featuring Harold Arlen
- **stormy weather** Ethel Waters
- **shadow waltz** Bing Crosby
- **lazybones** Ted Lewis
- **love is the sweetest thing** Ray Noble
- **the last round-up** George Olsen
- **the last round-up** Guy Lombardo
- **did you ever see a dream walking** Eddy Duchin

DUKE ELLINGTON AND HIS ORCHESTRA VISITED EUROPE FOR THE FIRST TIME.

The repeal of Prohibition stimulated the opening of thousands of bars and cocktail lounges around the country. Many were equipped with jukeboxes, creating a major new market for records.

IRVING BERLIN'S SCORE FOR THE BROADWAY HIT ***AS THOUSANDS CHEER*** INCLUDED THE TWO POP CLASSICS "EASTER PARADE" AND "HEAT WAVE."

BILLIE HOLLIDAY put out her first record this year, with Benny Goodman.

fiction

1. **anthony adverse**
   hervey allen
2. **as the earth turns**
   gladys hasty carroll
3. **ann vickers**
   sinclair lewis
4. **magnificent obsession**
   lloyd c. douglas
5. **one more river**
   john galsworthy
6. **forgive us our trespasses**
   lloyd c. douglas
7. **the master of jalna**
   mazo de la roche
8. **miss bishop**
   bess streeter aldrich
9. **the farm**
   louis bromfield
10. **little man, what now?**
    hans fallada

bestselling

Lifting the ban on **James Joyce**'s masterpiece ***Ulysses,*** the judge wrote that the book was "in many places . . . emetic . . . nowhere aphrodisiac."

nonfiction

1. **life begins at forty**
   walter b. pitkin
2. **marie antoinette**
   stefan zweig
3. **british agent**
   r. h. bruce lockhart
4. **100,000,000 guinea pigs**
   arthur kallet and f. j. schlink
5. **the house of exile**
   nora waln
6. **van loon's geography**
   hendrik willem van loon
7. **looking forward**
   franklin d. roosevelt
8. **contract bridge blue book of 1933**
   ely culbertson
9. **the arches of the years**
   halliday sutherland
10. **the march of democracy, vol. II**
    james truslow adams

AS WOODROW WILSON HAD DONE TWO DECADES EARLIER, FDR BEGAN HIS ADMINISTRATION WITH A BESTSELLING BOOK OUTLINING HIS POLICIES.

Exposure books, tomes that ripped the lid off their chosen subject, were introduced this year with Kallet and Schlink's treatise on the many false and misleading claims of modern advertising. Their work paved the way for other exposure-type books and gave an early boost to the still nascent consumer awareness movement.

Louis Meyer, right, and his mechanic Lawron Harrison, left

In the Indy 500, Louis Meyer drove to victory.

IN BASEBALL

the first All-Star game ever played was held in Chicago's Comiskey Park. 47,600 fans watched the National League lose to the American League, 4–2.

In the World Series, it was the New York Giants over the Washington Senators, 4 games to 1.

IN THE FIRST NATIONAL FOOTBALL LEAGUE CHAMPIONSHIP, THE CHICAGO BEARS SQUEAKED PAST THE NEW YORK GIANTS 23–21 BEFORE A HOME TEAM CROWD.

IN PROFESSIONAL GOLF, GENE SARAZEN TOOK HIS THIRD PGA CHAMPIONSHIP.

Primo Carnera, dubbed "the Italian Alp," defeated champion Jack Sharkey to become Heavyweight Champion of the World on June 29. Some 31,000 fans in the Long Island City Bowl watched in shock as Sharkey caught a right and hit the canvas in the sixth round.

sports

IN HORSE RACING, BROKERS TIP TOOK THE KENTUCKY DERBY WITH JOCKEY D. MEADE IN THE SADDLE.

IN TENNIS, IT WAS JACK CRAWFORD REIGNING AT **WIMBLEDON** FOR MEN. HELEN WILLS MOODY TOOK ANOTHER TITLE IN THE WOMEN'S COMPETITION.

notable films

State Fair, with Janet Gaynor and Will Rogers

Little Women, with Katharine Hepburn and Joan Bennett

Duck Soup, with the Marx Brothers

Footlight Parade, with James Cagney and Joan Blondell

Forty-second Street, with Ruby Keeler and Dick Powell

Gold Diggers of 1933, with Dick Powell and Joan Blondell

Dinner at Eight, with John and Lionel Barrymore and Jean Harlow

Design for Living, with Gary Cooper and Fredric March

The Invisible Man

IN *THE INVISIBLE MAN*, SPECIAL EFFECTS MADE **CLAUDE RAINES** INTO A HEADLESS, HANDLESS SET OF CLOTHES THAT KILLED.

Flying Down to Rio introduced Fred Astaire and Ginger Rogers, the new dance team that captivated America.

baby leroy, the 19-month-old movie star best known for his work opposite W. C. Fields, appeared before the camera in seven-minute segments for two hours a day. Baked potatoes and zwieback were among his favorite foods.

In *SHE DONE HIM WRONG*, **MAE WEST** introduced the line—"Come up and see me some time"—that made her famous.

WALT DISNEY PICKED UP AN OSCAR FOR THE CARTOON ***THE THREE LITTLE PIGS,*** THE FILM THAT ASKED THE MUSICAL QUESTION "WHO'S AFRAID OF THE BIG BAD WOLF?"

king kong brought to the screen the latest in special effects technology. The ape looked huge on screen, but filmmakers revealed that he was actually only 18 inches high.

oscar winners

Best Picture ***Cavalcade***

Best Actor **Charles Laughton,** *The Private Life of Henry VIII*

Best Actress **Katharine Hepburn,** *Morning Glory*

Best Director **Frank Lloyd,** *Cavalcade*

movies

King Kong

'33

Automakers touted gasoline mileage as a selling point. Drivers were more concerned than ever with economy.

This year's Pierce-Arrow Silver Arrow sedan featured a new, streamlined body with fastback roofline and slab sides. The car was the season's most talked-about new design, conceived by Phil

cars

ON THE SAFETY FRONT, MANY MANUFACTURERS NOW OFFERED OPTIONAL POWER BRAKES.

Wright. The vehicle, which was made mostly by hand, reached a dazzling speed of 115 mph and boasted a 175 horsepower V-12 engine.

aerodynamic streamlining

was a prominent feature of the National Automobile Show this year. The slanted windshield and the V-front grille both made appearances.

"STOP-LIGHTS" WERE OFFERED AS AN OPTION FOR THE FIRST TIME, ALONG WITH INDIVIDUAL WHEEL SUSPENSION AND PATENTED "NO DRAFT VENTILATION."

Women's fashion took tips from Hollywood this year. Stylish ladies took to the Garbo look, doffing the new "man's" evening suit. In the makeup department, it was Joan Crawford who set the look with bright lips, eye shadow, and artificial eyelashes.

'33

corsets played a big part in women's wear this season, creating the trendy V shape, dominated by wide shoulders, a small waist, and flared skirt.

fashion

Chanel raised eyebrows this year with its all-satin suit.

BOLERO JACKETS and **PUFF SLEEVES** made fashion headlines, along with short, fitted sweaters in solids or stripes.

IN A TOUCH OF EXOTICA, ADVENTUROUS LADIES DUSTED THEIR HAIR WITH PHOSPHORESCENT POWDER IN BRIGHT COLORS.

Enter: the Slim Tunic And Straighter Skirts

6688—Frock. Here's the new tunic silhouette. Be the first in your set to wear it—it does marvelous things for your figure. Designed for 14 to 46. For 16—3½ yards 39-inch light material, ⅝ yard dark. Width about 1⅝ yard.

6705—Frock. There's no need for dieting to wear the new frocks. Here's a smart model that takes inches from your silhouette. Designed for 34 to 52. For 34—4 yards 36-inch material, ½ yard dark. Width about 2⅜ yards.

6706—Frock. Point up your shoulders with "mousquetaire" sleeves and add a few buttons for trimmings—they're the very last word. Designed for 14 to 42. For 16—4½ yards 39-inch material. Width about 1¾ yard.

6664   6662

6664—Frock and Jacket Ensemble. Chic in the 1933 manner means slim, straight lines broken by a contrasting jacket in tunic effect. Designed for 14 to 42. For 16—3½ yards 39-inch dark material, 3⅝ yards 36-inch light. Width about 1⅝ yard.

6662—Frock and Coat Ensemble. Very Parisian. Designed for 12 to 42. For 16—2½ yards 54-inch material. 3½ yards 39-inch lining for coat, 2⅜ yards 39-inch plain material, ¾ yard 39-inch plaid for frock. Width about 1½ yard.

6688 6705 6706 6664 6662

final factoid

A new kind of doll was all the rage. Dubbed **dy-dee-doll,** it could "drink" a bottle of water and then wet itself. Sales were brisk.

credits

archive photos: inside front cover, pages 1, 5, 15, 21, 25, inside back cover

associated press: pages 2, 3, 4, 13, 16

photofest: pages 6, 8, 9, 10, 18, 19

gaslight: pages 7, 23

photo research:
alice albert

coordination:
rustyn birch

design:
carol bokuniewicz design
mutsumi hyuga